The HOW-TO's of Life!
How to STAY SAFE!

featuring

Illustrated by Cecilia Coto

MEET THE CHARACTERS!

Sophie, a pink elephant, is very kind but extremely shy. She is often afraid of new situations and finds meeting new people difficult. Sophie is insecure about her unique, pink appearance.

Sparkelina®, a young girl, is the wisest of the group. She has spent many years observing children and is a patient and loving mentor to her friends Busybee and Sophie.

Busybee, a giant bee, is goodhearted, energetic, and impulsive. As a bee, he is used to flying freely from place to place and has a hard time understanding etiquette and rules.

Original Title: How to Stay Safe!

Text: Kinderwise®
First Edition, March 2018

Illustrations: Cecilia Coto
Printed in U.S.A.

Copyright © 2018 by Kinderwise®
ALL RIGHTS RESERVED.

ISBN 978-0-9987115-4-6

DEDICATED TO MY SON JOEY, WITH LOVE

All rights reserved. No part of this publication, including but not limited to the content, illustrations, and names such as Sparkelina and Kinderwise may be reproduced, stored in a retrieval system, or transmitted in any form or by any means, electronic, mechanical, photocopying, recording or otherwise, without prior written permission of the publisher. Unauthorized use or reproduction of any aspect of this publication is strictly prohibited and may result in legal action. For permissions, email creator and publisher via kinderwise@gmail.com.

SUGGESTED READING METHODS:

1. After reading the book, ask your child to think of additional ways to stay safe.

2. Ask your child what they would do in each of the situations portrayed in the book.

3. Has your child encountered any of these dangers? Which ones?

4. Can you think of positive safety approaches you already take?

5. Are there any recent experiences you have had that could have been handled in a safer way?

6. An effective way of reinforcing these lessons is to use the character names when teaching. For example, instead of "The stove is hot; please stand back," you can try "Remember what happened to Busybee when he touched the stove?" This approach forces the child to think in more detail about the consequence of the action.

These are just suggestions. Be creative with your topics!

NOT SAFE

Cars can hurt you.

Always cross the street at a crosswalk with an adult.

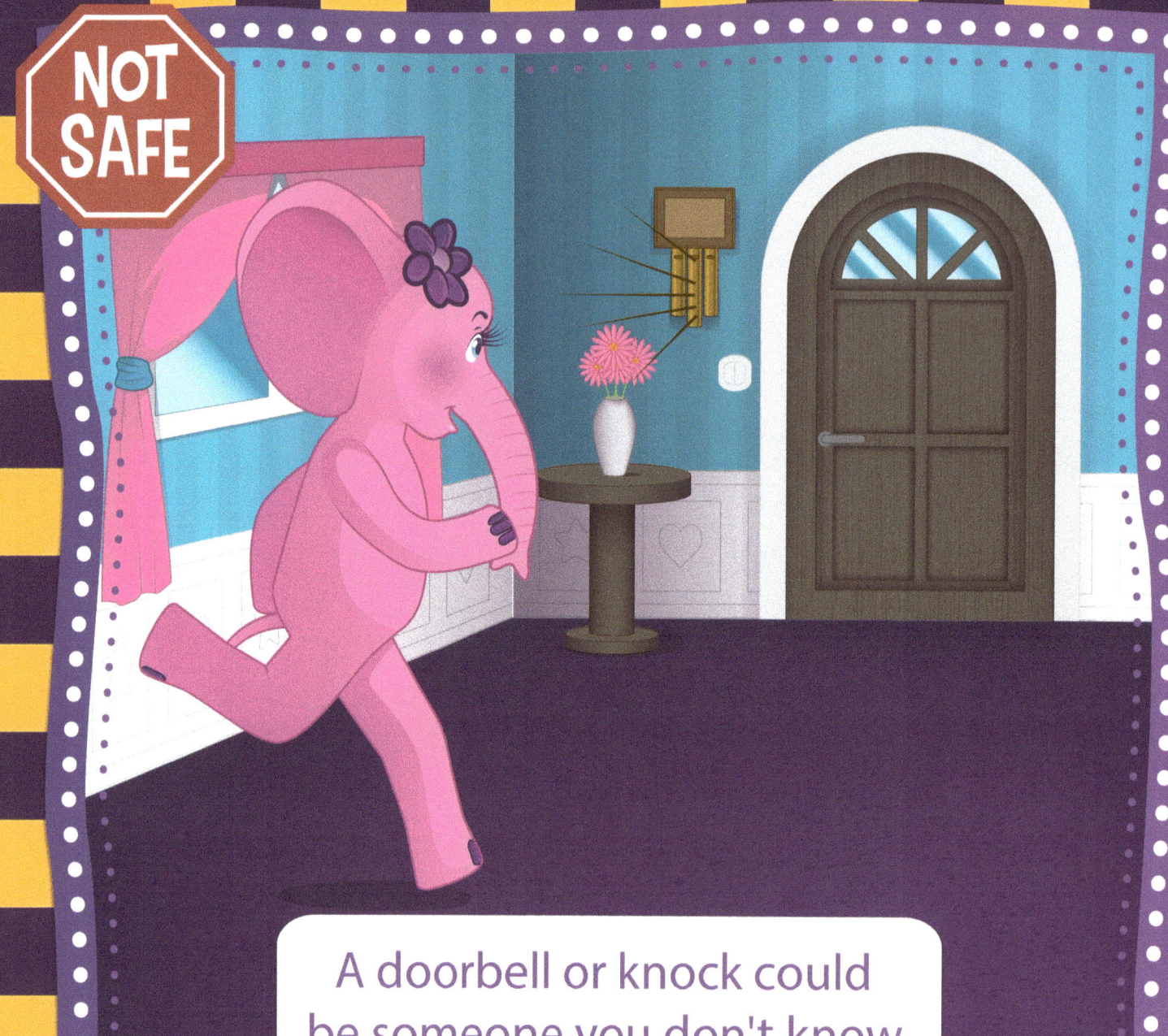

Tell an adult in your home if someone is at the door.

Adults should never come near if mom or dad isn't around.

Keep close to people you know and stay away from strangers.

Being lost in a crowd is scary.

Hold hands and stay together.

SAFETY TIPS FROM SPARKELINA

SAFETY TIP #1:

When lost in a crowd find a policeman and ask for help.

SAFETY TIP #2:

If an adult needs help or if you see smoke, dial 911.

SAFETY TIP #3:
Know your home address and your parents' phone numbers.

_____
Home Address

_____
Mom's phone number

_____
Dad's phone number

_____
Other

_____
Other

ABOUT KINDERWISE®

Kinderwise® and characters were founded by a dedicated mother based in Southern California who recognized the importance of teaching children essential life skills in a memorable way. With a focus on emotional intelligence, she created an acclaimed book series entitled "Emotional Intelligence Program for Children" and other educational products "The HOW-TO's of LIFE" featuring her beloved characters Sparkelina® (a young girl), Busybee (a giant bee), and Sophie (a pink elephant). Together, these characters navigate the challenges of the world, learning valuable lessons in a delightful and engaging manner. Kinderwise® and characters aim to provide children with a fun and interactive learning experience, fostering personal growth and development.

Why an emotional intelligence book series? The desire for a clear, accessible approach to emotional intelligence development stemmed from the personal experience of the female founder of Kinderwise®. Raised by an orphaned mother with Asperger syndrome and a highly intelligent, yet anti-social father, she found childhood social interaction to be a challenge. She read book after book to "fill in the blanks" of her own lack of social knowledge. She discovered that empathy, awareness of feelings, self-regulation and people skills form the foundation for a successful, happy life.

This guide can be used to re-enforce the daily life lessons that the founder taught her own son. She felt it was important that the book be written from the perspective of a child. To do this, she created three imaginary friends. Much like children, these characters would have to learn how to get along with each other and others. *The How-To's of Life!* book series was born.

Your support helps Kinderwise® to continue creating educational books aimed at helping children develop essential social skills. For more information, email: kinderwise@gmail.com